Dear Parent:
Your child's love of reading starts here!

Every child learns to read in a different way and at his or her own speed. Some go back and forth between reading levels and read favorite books again and again. Others read through each level in order. You can help your young reader improve and become more confident by encouraging his or her own interests and abilities. From books your child reads with you to the first books he or she reads alone, there are I Can Read Books for every stage of reading:

SHARED READING
Basic language, word repetition, and whimsical illustrations, ideal for sharing with your emergent reader

BEGINNING READING
Short sentences, familiar words, and simple concepts for children eager to read on their own

READING WITH HELP
Engaging stories, longer sentences, and language play for developing readers

READING ALONE
Complex plots, challenging vocabulary, and high-interest topics for the independent reader

ADVANCED READING
Short paragraphs, chapters, and exciting themes for the perfect bridge to chapter books

I Can Read Books have introduced children to the joy of reading since 1957. Featuring award-winning authors and illustrators and a fabulous cast of beloved characters, I Can Read Books set the standard for beginning readers.

A lifetime of discovery begins with the magical words **"I Can Read!"**

Visit www.icanread.com for information on enriching your child's reading experience.

*Ree Drummond and Diane deGroat gratefully
acknowledge the editorial and artistic contributions
of Amanda Glickman and Rick Whipple.*

I Can Read Book® is a trademark of HarperCollins Publishers.

Charlie the Ranch Dog: Charlie's Snow Day Text copyright © 2013 by Ree Drummond. Cover art copyright © 2013 by Diane deGroat. Interior art copyright © 2013 by HarperCollins Publishers. All rights reserved. Manufactured in China. No part of this book may be used or reproduced in any manner whatsoever without written permission except in the case of brief quotations embodied in critical articles and reviews. For information address HarperCollins Children's Books, a division of HarperCollins Publishers, 10 East 53rd Street, New York, NY 10022.
www.icanread.com

Library of Congress catalog card number: 2012956497
ISBN 978-0-06-221912-1 (trade bdg.) —ISBN 978-0-06-221911-4 (pbk.)

13 14 15 16 17 SCP 10 9 8 7 6 5 4 3 2 1 ❖ First Edition

I Can Read!™

BEGINNING 1 READING

CHARLIE
the Ranch Dog
CHARLIE'S SNOW DAY

based on the CHARLIE THE RANCH DOG books
by REE DRUMMOND, The Pioneer Woman
and DIANE deGROAT

HARPER
An Imprint of HarperCollinsPublishers

Yawn.

Good morning.

Hey! Check it out!

Everything is white outside.

It's snow!

I'd better go and tell Mama.

Am I going to stay inside all day?

That doesn't sound like much fun!

Sniff, sniff.

Someone is on the porch.

It's Mama!

Walter and I follow Mama

across the pasture,

to the big hill.

My big sister is at the tippy top.

She is sitting on a sled.

"Yahoo!" she shouts,

and flies down the hill.

She is going so fast!

I want to try, too.

I bet I can go even faster.

"Come on," I say to Walter.

Together, we take a running start.

I'll show him how it's done!

WHOOSH!

The snow sprays my nose.

My ears flap in the wind.

This is great!

Walter and I slip and slide
faster and faster.

Uh-oh.

How will we stop?

CRASH!

We smash into a pile of fluffy
snow.

Wow! That was fun!

I can't wait to go again!

I look up and see my sister

on top of the hill.

The hill looks bigger from below.

It looks like a big, tall mountain!

I start to go up.

And up.

And up.

Pant, pant.

My paws skid on the icy slope.

Cold, wet snow sticks to my fur.

My ears aren't very floppy

anymore.

They are frozen stiff!

This is no fun.

Finally, I get to the top.

I don't want to play outside anymore.

All I want is a nap in the warm house!

Walter wants to go again.

What's wrong with that guy?

There is no way I am ever

climbing up that hill again.

WHIR! Walter sprays snow

everywhere.

WHOOSH! Sister glides by on her sled.

ZIP! Daddy and Mama fly by.

I give everyone "the look."

Everyone is having a blast

except me.

I'm cold!

"Walter!" I hear Sister cry out.

Huh?

Where IS Walter?

Sniff, sniff!

I catch a whiff of Walter,

but I don't see him anywhere.

He could be in big trouble.

He could be trapped under the snow!

ZOOM!

I take off

faster than a rocket.

RRRRRRROOOWW-OOOOOH!

I howl so Walter knows I'm coming.

Okay, and because I love to howl.

Sniff, sniff!

I follow my nose.

I dig through a giant mound of snow.

Walter! There you are!

Walter gives my face a huge lick.

Mama, Daddy, and Sister run over.

I stare at the steep, slippery hill.

It will be a long slog back up.

But it was worth it to save Walter.

Hands reach down and scoop me up.

Mama puts me on a sled.

Daddy and Sister drag me behind them.

Now this is more like it!

Up and up we go.

I see the house

and think of my warm, cozy bed.

Maybe Mama will even make bacon!